... can we write it as a play?

A BOOK OF PLAYWRITING IDEAS FOR USE IN SCHOOLS

Barry Simner

Hodder & Stoughton

A MEMBER OF THE HODDER HEADLINE GROUP

Acknowledgements

The authors and publishers would like to thank the following for their kind permission to reproduce copyright material:

Robert Walker, Matthew Foster and Chris Wallace at the Wirral Grammar School for Boys.

Faber and Faber Ltd for extract from *The Dumb Waiter* by Harold Pinter; *The Observer* for 'Deaf gunman snapped over late Giro' by Alex Starmer; HMSO for extract from *A Language for Life* (DES, 1975); V. S. Naipaul for extract from *The Enigma of Arrival*

Every effort has been made to trace and acknowledge ownership of copyright. The Publishers will be glad to make suitable arrangements with any copyright holders whom they have been unable to contact.

British Library Cataloguing in Publication Data

A catalogue for this title is available from the British Library.

ISBN 0340 55927 6

First published 1994
Impression number 10 9 8 7 6 5 4 3 2
Year   1999 1998 1997 1996 1995

Typeset by Wearset, Boldon, Tyne and Wear.
Printed in UK for the educational publishing division of Hodder & Stoughton Ltd., a division of Hodder Headline Plc, 338 Euston Road, London NW1 3BH by Athenaeum Press Ltd, Team Valley, Gateshead.

CONTENTS

Dedication

I owe a debt of gratitude to: Penny Cherns for her help and encouragement; the teachers in Gwynedd, Powys and Dyfed who gave me the opportunity to devise these classes and to the students who took part in the workshop sessions.

In particular I have to thank Andy Hawkins, English Advisor for Powys, for inviting me to her inspiring A level English creative writing weekends.

Barry Simner
Llanegryn
January 1994

INTRODUCTION

———

Ask a class to write a story, and there will always be someone who puts up a hand and says, 'Can we write it as a play?'

Young people *like* plays. They like reading them and they like writing them. We shouldn't be surprised at this; after all, the 'play' in the shape of endless television series, soap operas and films is probably the narrative form with which they are now most familiar.

But this question, 'Can we write it as a play?', often disguises a secret appeal and can mean: 'I don't really want to write *anything*. I'm prepared to give this a go, but I don't want to be bothered with speech marks, paragraphs, character descriptions or long descriptive passages. Above all, I don't want to write a plan first. So I'll write a play instead. Okay?'

Likewise, our acquiescence may contain its own subtext: 'You haven't written a thing this term; your folder has to be in in three weeks; it's Friday; I'm tired, and if you want to write a play instead of a story, that's fine. Just so long as you write *something*.'

The classroom is an environment rich in such covert deals, and this one would matter no more than any other, if the results were not always so uniformly disappointing – little more than rambling dialogue without direction or structure. For pupils, writing a play seems to be an easy option, the formless form that requires no planning and the minimum of effort.

I think it's a shame to allow dramatic writing to fall into such disrepute. Simply because drama is a familiar form to our pupils does not mean that plays can be written without some effort or knowledge of the skills and techniques of the dramatist.

Contrary to popular belief, playwrights don't *write* plays: they *make* them. 'Wright' comes from the Old English word for a craftsman, a maker. Making a play is a unique activity which involves a range of skills and unusual methods of writing, and once we have thought of a play as something fashioned and constructed (rather than the spontaneous outpouring of feeling or opinion) we can begin to think about the sort of skills our pupils will need.

It is on this neglected area of creative writing that this book attempts to focus. It is a collection of ideas that grew out of some classes I gave to sixth-form students in Wales. They were studying English at Advanced level, and one of the requirements of the course was that they should write some sort of script. They were enthusiastic and they had lots of ideas, but they weren't sure how to get started. Their teachers asked if I would help.

I began by looking at my own experience as a writer and realised that I certainly hadn't begun writing plays with a set of rules by my side. This book didn't exist, and the couple of books I did look at which were supposed to teach me how to write a play did nothing of the kind: they gave me plenty of rules, but they didn't tell me what I really wanted to know – how to get started.

Experience of other kinds of writing had, however, taught me that the most interesting things I wrote happened when I surprised myself: when I said things I didn't know I wanted to say, in ways in which I didn't know I wanted to say them. In other words, the best writing seemed always to be a process of discovery.

This will not actually help the young person who wants to know how to get started, but it nevertheless provided the starting point for this book. What I wanted to do was to introduce pupils to the *process* of writing by providing them with a range of activities over which they would be unable to exercise total control. By placing them in a position in which they knew neither the outcome nor the route by which they were to arrive at it, I hoped to introduce them to the excitement and the enjoyment of writing. After all, pupils who have experienced the thrill and pleasure of writing are unlikely to have any difficulty 'getting started'.

Just in case all this sounds merely indulgent, we should not forget that writing plays also features prominently in the programme of study for English (AT1). And, if further pedagogical justification for this process of writing is required, what can be more apposite than this quotation, taken from the 1975 Bullock report into the teaching of English?

> '... the evidence is that one acquires language as a *pattern*, not as an inert collection of units added serially, a mechanical accumulation of abstract parts of speech ... language competence grows *incrementally*, through an interaction of writing, talk, reading and experience, the body of work forming an organic whole.'

> (HMSO, 1975 – *my italics*)

HOW TO USE THIS BOOK

This book is aimed principally at the teacher; it comprises a number of 'chapters' (each based on a central exercise), some of which examine underlying structures and conventions. Each of the exercises is entirely self-contained and tries to approach an aspect of playwriting from an unusual and original angle. All involve group work or an element of collaboration, and the aim is to get pupils to the point where they feel confident enough to write independently.

The chapters provide a brief account of the genesis of the idea, practical advice and step-by-step instructions, some theoretical points and suggestions for follow-up work. Little or nothing is required by way of preparation. Each exercise could last one hour or one week, provide a single 'one-off' lesson in a moment of panic or form the basis for a whole term's work. It all depends on the enthusiasm of the class and the inventiveness of the teacher.

This is not an instruction manual or a complete course in playwriting. The ideas are not in any sense a set of prescriptions which will tell you how to teach your pupils how to write a play. You do not have to start at the beginning of the book and work through to the end, nor do you have to do all the exercises.

My advice is to allow the lesson to unfold rather than to try to force things to a predetermined conclusion – not always easy to follow in these days of attainment targets, assessments and reviews. If you think that by doing A, B and C your class will end up with a play, you are bound to be disappointed with the book. By all means work through the different chapters towards that end, but feel free to use them independently to provide practice in the writing of dialogue or the creation of character in other forms of narrative.

Finally, most of my own experience as a writer has been in television, and there is a natural bias in the book towards television drama. The television drama is a very different piece of work from the stage play, although there are similarities. When I write of the 'play', therefore, I am using the term in an imprecise way to mean any dramatic writing done with performance in mind.

1. 'INSIDE OUT' PLAYS

Language is social behaviour, and plays are made from what people say to one another. Unlike the novel or short story, talk in a play has an enormous amount to do: it must reveal character and it must carry the narrative and the plot forward.

A play, of course, is not real life, and people in the real world do not speak like people on stage or television. Nevertheless, good realistic speech in a play should have something of the spontaneity and unexpectedness of the most interesting everyday speech. One way to do this is to encourage pupils to start eavesdropping.

In Old English, the word 'eavesdrop' described the dripping of water from the overhanging roof of a house. If you stood within the space where the roof overhung the wall – the eavesdrop – you could not only keep dry, you could also listen in secret to the private conversation of the people inside the house.

This is not to suggest that your pupils should deliberately set out to invade the privacy of other people, but in our crowded society it's often difficult not to overhear what others are saying. For the playwright, the fragments of conversation picked up in this way can be extremely helpful. Even when these snatches of speech seem nonsensical there is always a temptation to try to make sense of them – to invent a story or a character and put what one hears into a context.

Often a chance remark will give a vivid impression of a character, part of a story or an insight into a strange and different sort of life. One such example occurred to me recently: I was on a London bus, just after the morning rush hour. There were a lot of elderly people on the bus, and they were talking about how much things had changed since they were children and how violent society now was. After a short pause one man said, 'You see … the thing is … years ago … during the war … we never had any of this violence then.'

 As proof that even good dialogue, professionally performed, is still a long way from real speech, try the following experiment.

1

Pre-set your radio to Radio 4. Turn on the set for two or three seconds so that you get a snatch of conversation and then turn it off again. Ask yourself whether what you heard was 'real' people talking or actors. Check by turning on again.

Nine times out of ten you will always be able to tell actors from real people. Why? Vocal quality has something to do with it (actors on radio often sound too much like actors), as do atmosphere and subject, but the principal reason is that actors always know what they are going to say next. In everyday life we seldom know what we are going to say. We may have a rough 'agenda', but we're never quite sure how we're going to speak it. Even very good actors have trouble trying to make a script sound as fresh and surprising as real speech.

Pupils should be encouraged to pay attention to what they and others *actually* say to one another in real life and not rely on what they *think* they say and hear. Stilted dialogue is dialogue which has no muscle or sinew; it is speech in which speakers say exactly what they mean all the time, speech without the sense of danger that comes from not quite knowing what is going to come out of your mouth next.

Listening, recording and transcribing can help pupils develop an 'ear' for the richness, spontaneity, humour and rhythm of real speech.

EXERCISE

The aim of the following exercise is to show:

- how compelling is the need to impose meaning on random utterance,

- the ease with which an entire 'scene' can be created from one very brief exchange,

- that the 'turn-taking' nature of normal conversation does not mean that dialogue in a play need be written sequentially. It is possible, sometimes essential, to start a scene in the middle and work outwards. That is where this exercise begins.

Instructions

Each of the following exchanges between A and B is really a very short play, possibly the shortest plays ever written. (Having said that, there is a set of even shorter exchanges given later in this chapter on p.6, which I have at times found an even better starting point for this exercise.)

A: Go on! Have a small one.
B: I won't be able to drive if I do.

A: It started in my neck, but now it's gone down here.
B: I should see a doctor if I were you.

A: If you ask me, he had it coming.
B: Well, I feel sorry for him.

A: Oh darling, is it really ours?
B: Yes, but we've still got to pay for it.

A: We're just good friends.
B: Do you really expect me to believe that?

A: They're very funny people round here.
B: That's what I'm worried about.

A: It's the same thing every year.
B: Maybe we should try EuroDisney for a change.

A: I wanted a green one, but he likes blue.
B: Why not compromise?

A: This one looks interesting.
B: It's much too heavy to take on holiday.

A: It hasn't moved for the last five minutes.
B: Read the instructions again.

A: I wouldn't wish this on my worst enemy.
B: Just sit still and it might go away.

A: That one looks completely worn out.
B: I think he had a late night.

A: Do you mind if we have the window open?
B: As long as I don't get a stiff neck.

A: That last one was a bit low.
B: You're not kidding! It nearly hit me.

A: Are you sure he's asleep?
B: I suppose he could be dead.

A: I think it's for you.
B: I wasn't expecting a visitor.

A: I don't think it fits properly.
B: You look wonderful in it.

A: You know I hate Sundays.
B: You'll just have to make an effort.

Cut the plays up into individual lines so that you are left with one pile of A lines and one pile of B lines (I put them into separate, marked envelopes). Seat the group in a circle and divide the pupils up alternately into As and Bs (A, B, A, B, A, B ... and so on). Explain that you are giving them all one line of a very short play for two people and that in every 'play' A opens the exchange and B always replies. Then give all the As an A line and all the Bs a B line.

The element of surprise is important. Ask the group, without rehearsal and without showing their sentences to their partner, to read their 'plays' around the circle. Some of the exchanges will already seem to make sense, while others will be simply bizarre.

Now ask each person to find the other half of their 'play' by trying their line out on as many other people in the group as possible. The important thing is that pupils find someone with whom their line seems to work, however odd the result. In fact it's much more interesting if the lines *don't* match in the way they do here on the page. One way of ensuring this is to have more 'plays' than pupils. The ones who can't find a partner must make do with whoever's left; these will often turn out to be the most productive and interesting of all.

Once all pupils have found a partner, each pair should read the result to the rest of the group. I usually listen to all of them, making passing remarks on each, before going on to a more detailed discussion about which of the 'plays' we like best and why.

Very often a strong sense of place or character, which may not always be apparent to the performers, will come across immediately. This is a good point at which to discuss if and why the 'plays' seem to work, e.g.:

- Are we imposing a meaning on them?
- If so, do we all agree on the meaning?
- Does what the 'audience' thinks bear any relation to what the authors thought was happening?

Next, ask the group, again working in pairs, to expand their plays by writing two more lines, one for A (to go after the original B line) and one for B (to go before the original A line) – it's a good idea to have pupils write the two original lines out in the middle of a page so that there is room for the play to expand. The groups 'top and tail' the original two-line 'play' in this way, so that what began as A B becomes B A B A. The next step is to add two more lines top and bottom so that we get A B A B A B, and so on, as in this example.

A: Hi!
B: What are you doing?

A: I'm trying to build a universe.
B: How's it going?
A: It hasn't moved for the last five minutes.
B: Read the instructions again.
A: They're in Japanese.
B: Are the batteries in the right way?
A: I don't think it needs any.
B: Mine did. Perhaps it's a later model.

Robert Walker

At some point it may prove difficult to go any further without deciding who is speaking and where the scene is taking place. More likely a sense of character and place will begin to emerge as the dialogue grows. Whatever happens, this is a crucial stage and worth examining in detail, for example:

- At exactly what point do you begin to think of A or B as a person?

- Where do you begin to get some idea of where these people are?

Indications of character and situation will often be signalled by quite small details, a word or two which the audience will use as evidence of some particular trait or location. Far from being an example of our 'reading something into' the dialogue, this is a perfectly legitimate strategy and can provide an important lesson in the creation of character and place, i.e. that it is not necessary to know what your character had for breakfast in order to make her convincing.

One interesting thing that I've discovered is that, if you try adding another line from your collection to your two existing lines, the exercise becomes much more difficult. I think this is because it relies for its effect on the element of surprise. For the same reason, the most bizarre pairs of lines often work best.

Follow-up suggestions

1. Ask the group to reflect on how they wrote their scene:

- What clues did they find in the original lines?

- Was it necessary to take turns or was it possible to jump ahead and work backwards?

- What were the limitations of the form?

- At what point, if any, did they have to make definite decisions about character and setting?

- Alternatively, did character and setting emerge naturally as they went on?
- Did any sort of narrative begin to appear and, if so, how?

The point to remember is that students need to be sensitive to both what they are doing and how they are doing it. They should be encouraged to become their own experts.

2. If the group is interested, it's worth pushing the exercise further by using as the starting point brief exclamations or single words instead of whole sentences. Some teachers may find that these single words make a better introduction to the whole exercise. It is not so easy to 'pair off' these words and exclamations, and they may therefore serve better to illustrate our ability to construct a coherent context, plot and characters out of apparently disparate materials.

Here are some examples of single words or exclamations that you could use:

A: Sshh.
B: What?
A: Ouch!
B: No.
A: Please.
B: Hmph.
A: Really?
B: Mmm.
A: So?
B: Okay.
A: Tut.
B: Phew!
A: Aha.
B: Dadaa!
A: Go.
B: Wait.
A: Now?
B: Gently.
A: Shit!
B: Oh no.
A: Attention.
B: Stop.
A: Me?
B: You.
A: Help.
B: Why?

3. Pupils could start a collection of snatches of conversations overheard in school or on the street which they could bring back to the class with the aim of generating a piece of dialogue.

4. Pupils might, alternatively, try 'bibliomancy'. This involves opening a book anywhere, pointing to a section with their eyes closed, writing out the word, phrase or sentence under their finger and trying to use it somewhere in a dialogue.

5. You could record a genuine conversation between two speakers (with their permission) and extract from it one exchange. Ask the class to follow the previous exercise and then compare their written scenes with the original.

Remind pupils that the most boring people to talk to are those who have made up their minds about everything and are determined to press on with what they have to say regardless of anyone else. They are the people who never deviate and never allow us to influence them. When writing dialogue, we may know exactly where we want the scene to go but we have to write it as though we had no idea. Pupils should allow what their character says to have an effect, to modify the opinions of the other character and influence his replies, just as in the liveliest conversation between real people.

'Inside out plays' might help pupils write a dialogue that has something of the spontaneity and unexpectedness we find in real speech because neither of the writers know what's coming next: the intention, as in most writing, is revealed to the authors in and through the process.

2. AN ACT OF SPEECH

A play consists of characters talking to one another – trying to get things done with words. As in real life, these people are speaking for a purpose: they want to be rich and powerful; they want that man or that woman; they want to be loved; they want to be feared.

One of the things to bear in mind when writing a play is what the characters want. It may be a small 'want' restricted to one part of a scene: for example, in a scene from *An Inspector Calls*, Inspector Goole wants to know whether Mr Birling knows a woman called Eva Smith. It might, however, be a big 'want' that permeates everything the character does and says in the play: in the play just quoted, Inspector Goole wants to expose the hypocrisy of the whole Birling family and, through that, the hypocrisy of their entire class.

The linguist J L Austin, writing of the function of discourse (the way we use speech to get things done), uses the term 'speech act' to describe the function of an utterance. He lists more than a hundred possibilities, such as 'command', 'direct', 'request', 'question', etc.

Austin suggests that the purpose of an utterance may be:

- to get something done (for example, 'Put those plates away');

- to express a psychological state (for example, 'I can't take any more');

- or to commit the speaker to some course of action (for example, 'I'll come over when I've finished work').

Few people say exactly what they mean all the time, either in real life or in plays (life might be simpler if they did, but it would almost certainly be more painful), and the term 'subtext' was coined to differentiate between what is said and what is intended. However, before we get to the subtext we have to begin with what is said; in this respect, Austin's idea of speech acts might be useful.

In Harold Pinter's short play, *The Dumb Waiter*, Gus and Ben are waiting in the basement of a disused restaurant for the person they must kill. From the start there is a dangerous degree of tension between the two men. At first we don't know they are gunmen, but we do observe that they don't seem to trust each other. Gus cleverly manipulates his partner. He preys on Ben's insecurity, making him uneasy and angry until the final moments of the play when the situation is dramatically reversed.

The following is an exercise which involves a very simple analysis of some of the dialogue in this play. Photocopy this extract from the play and give it to your pupils. Their task is to define each part of the dialogue in terms of 'speech acts': the first few exchanges have been defined already.

[An envelope containing some matches has been pushed under the basement door. Gus and Ben have been examining them.]

BEN:	Don't waste them!	*Command*
	Go on, go and light it.	*Instruction*
GUS:	Eh?	*Query*
BEN:	Go and light it	*Instruction*
GUS:	Light what?	*Question*
BEN:	The kettle.	*Explanation*
GUS:	You mean the gas.	*Correction*
BEN:	Who does?	*Question*
GUS:	You do.	*Explanation*
BEN	(*his eyes narrowing*): What do you mean, I mean the gas?	*Question/Challenge*
GUS:	Well, that's what you mean, don't you? The gas?	*Question/Suggestion*
BEN	(*powerfully*): If I say go and light the kettle I mean go and light the kettle.	*Statement/Threat*

GUS: How can you light a kettle?

BEN: It's a figure of speech! Light the kettle. It's a figure of speech.

GUS: I've never heard of it.

BEN: Light the kettle! It's common usage!

GUS: I think you've got it wrong.

BEN   (*menacing*): What do you mean?

GUS: They say put on the kettle.

BEN   (*taut*): Who says?

[*They stare at each other, breathing hard.*]

BEN: (*deliberately*): I have never in all my life heard anyone say put on the kettle.

GUS: I bet my mother used to say it.

BEN: Your mother? When did you last see your mother?

GUS: I don't know, about –

BEN: Well, what are you talking about your mother for?

[*They stare.*]

BEN: Gus, I'm not trying to be unreasonable. I'm just trying to point out something to you.

GUS: Yes, but –

BEN: Who's the senior partner here, me or you?

GUS: You.

BEN: I'm only looking after your interests, Gus. You've got to learn, mate.

GUS: Yes, but I've never heard –

BEN   (*vehemently*): Nobody says light the gas! What does the gas light?

GUS: What does the gas – ?

BEN   (*grabbing with two hands by the throat, at arm's length*): THE KETTLE, YOU FOOL!

When pupils come to reflect on their attempts to define the exchanges in this extract, one of the things that should strike them is the number of questions that are asked: out of 31 lines 13 are questions of some sort. Gus begins this trend with his apparently innocent, 'Eh?', but most of the questions (eight) are Ben's. The purpose of Gus's original 'Eh?' seems to be to undermine Ben's composure rather than find something out. It is designed to rattle Ben so that he begins to feel insecure. His insecurity makes him turn on Gus and begin to interrogate him. Gus's wilful misunderstanding seems to place him in a position from which he can begin to control the situation.

Another of Gus's tactics is reminiscent of our first exercise in building scenes from fragments of conversation. Gus chooses to pick Ben up on one of those phrases we use everyday but which, in strictly logical terms, is nonsense: 'Light the kettle,' he says. Gus, the junior partner, takes Ben literally in order to undermine him: 'How can you light a kettle?'

EXERCISE

This next exercise turns Austin's method of analysis on its head. Here we begin with a description of the various speech acts and then use that description as a means of generating dialogue. In doing so, the aim is to make the nature of the conversation more explicit by drawing attention first to the underlying intention of the speaker. The idea is for pupils to work collaboratively from a set of given instructions to create a piece of original dialogue.

Instructions

Divide the group into As and Bs and ask each of them to write one line in response to the following instructions. They should not allow their partner to see what they are writing.

A: Greet B.

B: Request something from A.

A: Make a statement about the weather.

B: Ask a question.

A: Apologise.

B: Thank A.

A: Plead.

B: Deny something.

A: Accuse someone of something.

B: Suggest something.

A: Refuse a gift.

B: Pass a compliment.

A: Ridicule.

B: Threaten.

A: Defy.

B: Offer something.

A: Take offence.

B: Sympathise.

A: Congratulate.

B: Frighten.

A: Command.

B: Sneer.

A: Apologise.

B: Encourage.

A: Admit something.

B: Complain.

Each pupil should do this independently while nevertheless paying attention to *all* the instructions. A should allow the instructions given to B to influence her response and vice versa. For example, when B hears A being told to write a greeting, he should allow this to influence his request. And when A hears B being told to thank her, she should allow that to influence the sort of plea she makes.

Each line of the scene will now be a concrete version of the abstract instruction; you will have given the bald instructions some life.

When the whole list is complete, pupils should work in pairs, reading their lines alternately to one another and then redrafting and improving by making their efforts agree (tense of verbs, etc.).

Next, the results should be shared with the rest of the class and discussed. Pupils should pay particular attention to:

- the differences and similarities between the separate versions;

- the ease or difficulty with which the underlying structure can be perceived;

- what it is that makes many of them so funny.

This particular list was devised almost at random, but you might find that whatever structure there is will tend to generate scenes with a similar mood or atmosphere, regardless of what is actually said. Indeed, it would be interesting to see if we could reproduce the mood of the scene between Gus and Ben by following the same outline structure of questions, threats and statements which they use.

One such structure might be a straightforward set of questions and answers, but there are other possibilities. What sort of scene would emerge, for example:

- from a continuous exchange of statements?

- when every question is met by another question?

- when the exchange takes the form of constant accusations followed by denials?

Whatever structure is used, what is important is the examination of the underlying pattern of the dialogue and the manner in which it influences the dramatic shape of the scene.

Follow-up suggestions

1. Examine the results of the dialogues and try to work out exactly what strategies are being employed. See if it is possible to produce a different effect by altering the sequence of instructions. What happens when the whole sequence is reversed or parts exchanged? What happens if both participants end on a question, or on a statement of intent? How is the tone of the exchange affected when one speaker always repeats the previous line before answering?

2. Take an extract from a playtext, preferably a piece for two characters, and ask pupils to make their own analysis of the speech acts involved. They should be encouraged to use and develop their own terminology as far as possible before using this to create a new dialogue.

3. Ask pupils to write a short scene, either collaboratively or

independently, in which the two characters have a 'secret agenda'. A might secretly want to borrow some money from B but needs to disguise his intention. B might have heard that A is likely to turn violent at the slightest provocation and must be handled with sensitivity.

Analyse these scenes into their component 'speech acts' and try to get a clear picture of what each character is actually doing as the scene progresses.

4.   Ask pupils to write a scene between two charactes in which every opening 'move' by one is 'blocked' by the other. Following this pattern, questions would never be answered, observations never acknowledged, requests never met, appeals would always be denied and statements always gainsaid. This would be a useful technique to use if you were wanting to write a scene in which one character is humiliated or frustrated by someone else.

5.   Sometimes the subtext is the real purpose of the conversation, and often it is more interesting than what the characters appear to be saying. Pupils could attempt to write a piece of dialogue in which two characters *appear* to be talking about one topic when it is clear that they are really talking about something else: for example, the conversation might appear to be about the weather but in reality is about how one person loves or hates the other.

This is relatively easy in performance, where actors can use all their skills to communicate what cannot be spoken: it would be interesting to try to write such a conversation. One of the ways speakers draw attention to the subtext of their conversation is deliberately to subvert the normal conventions of speech. In order to make someone feel uncomfortable or insecure, for example, a speaker might follow a question with another question or a greeting with a statement about the state of one's health or the weather.

3. STORY AND PLOT

Before a story can become a play, it must first become a plot. In this respect, the plays of Shakespeare are no different from television plays: the author may begin with a *story*, but it must be fashioned into a *plot* before it can become drama. Aristotle called playwrights 'makers of plots'. For him, the plot was the most important element in a play – far more important than character; it is because pupils fail to grasp the difference between these two fundamental terms – which is that the story tells us *what* happened, and the plot tells us *why* – that their plays are so often unsatisfactory.

E M Forster put this clearly when he said that a story is 'a narrative of events arranged in their time sequence'. A plot, he says, 'is also a narrative of events, the emphasis falling on causality'. He gives an example of what he means: '"The king died and then the queen died" is a story. "The king died and then the queen died of grief" is a plot.'

In the plot there is a reason for what happens: the death of the queen has a *cause* – grief. Once we know that, we can start to construct a drama: the queen loved the king so much that, when he died, she could no longer go on living. Forster takes this plot a step further and says, '"The queen died, no one knew why, until it was discovered that it was through grief at the death of the king." This is a plot with a mystery in it, a form capable of high development.'

It is this crucial element of causality which creates drama. We don't just want to know what happens to the queen – we want to know why. The structure of a play is concerned with these two basic elements.

Finding the story

In *The Enigma of Arrival*, the novelist V S Naipaul talks about becoming a writer:

> '... the idea given to me by my education ... was that the writer was a person possessed of sensibility; that the writer was someone who recorded or displayed an inward development.... It was nearly five years before vision was

granted me, quite suddenly one day, when I was desperate for such an illumination, of what my material as a writer might be.... [I] saw that my subject was not my sensibility, my inward development, but the worlds I contained within myself, the worlds I lived in.'

The realisation that we already know our stories is a heartening discovery and can liberate us from self-obsession. Each one of us, in our own families and groups, knows stories as good as any we will ever see on stage or screen and characters more interesting and more complex than any we will meet in books. Finding the story begins by looking out there to the real world, not contemplating our own neurosis.

Some writers, like Italo Calvino, have expressed distaste for stories taken from real life, believing that they were plundering something sacred. But human beings are story-telling animals, and narrative, as Barbara Hardy has pointed out, seems to be a 'primary act of mind' with us. We cannot stop telling one another stories about ourselves.

How then does a story become a plot? The prerequisites for a playwright are inquisitiveness and an overwhelming interest in people: what do they do, and why do they do it? Writers must always be asking 'What?' and 'Why?' Why did that man hurt that man? What was the cause of that woman's misery?

When we begin to answer some of these questions we are on our way to making a plot.

 As an example of how an incident can become a story, and then a plot, simply by asking the right sort of questions, let's look at the following.

At 9.15 one morning, police are called to a road traffic accident. They find a woman injured by a motorcycle that hit her as she was crossing the road. An ambulance arrives. The woman, who's not badly hurt, tells the police that the accident was her fault because she didn't look where she was going. She says she's given the motorcyclist her address. The motorcyclist is also uninjured, but his bike is a 'write-off'. The police learn that he was on his way to work and that the woman was collecting her benefit from the DSS. The ambulance crew say they want to take her to hospital: she says she's in a hurry to get home and refuses to go. She agrees to allow the police to drive her home, but, when they get there, she won't let them into the house to make sure that she is all right.

So far this is a simple narrative of events arranged in a time sequence. It tells us exactly what happens, but it doesn't tell us *why*. I think there is one central 'why?' in this: why doesn't she want police in her house?

Maybe her husband is a thief and the house is full of stolen goods. Maybe she has an escaped convict in hiding. Maybe she just doesn't like policemen. These are all answers, but they're not very interesting answers. A more interesting solution may be this: Liz Kirby (let's give her a name) is an unregistered child-minder and, if the police find out, she could be prosecuted.

This leads us to another question: why was she in such a hurry to get home? Answer: she had left her children alone in the house while she went out to collect her benefit.

Suddenly our incident begins to look interesting: now that we have answered the central question 'why?', we begin to see other questions and other possibilities. Liz Kirby is child-minding and claiming benefit: is she greedy or desperate?

Before answering that question, let's consider another point about this incident that isn't immediately obvious. Motorcyclists, like all road users, must have insurance: pedestrians do not. Therefore, our motorcyclist (let's call him Robert Jones) cannot claim money for the damage to his machine from the person who caused the accident, Liz Kirby. What could he do about this?

He could take a civil court action for damages, but that takes a long time. He could claim off his own insurance, but that would mean losing his no-claims bonus. Remember that he has Kirby's address. My answer? He goes to her home and threatens to hurt her if she doesn't give him the money to repair his bike.

Now that we have asked and answered a couple of questions, we can begin to turn this simple story into a plot. Our main difficulty is going to be allowing the police to find out what's going on. Here's my solution:

Called to an accident, PC Andrews and WPC Steeds find Liz Kirby, thirty-five, injured by a motorcyclist, Robert Jones: she admits to carelessness on her way to collect DSS benefit. Anxious to get home, she accepts a lift from police while Jones is left moaning about his damaged bike. Andrews and Steeds are puzzled by Kirby's refusal of further help. Later, a neighbour of Kirby's calls police saying she's heard an argument and seen a man leaving Kirby's flat; now children are screaming. Andrews and Steeds find Kirby frightened and in tears and looking after four children she says belong to friends. She says she's had a visit from Jones who's forced her to sign an IOU for £1000 to cover damage to his bike. They decide to have a word with Jones. As they are leaving, they meet a woman who collects her children and pays Liz. Liz admits she's child-minding for cash and is unregistered. The police ask her what time the children are delivered to her in the morning, and she says 8 o'clock. Liz has to admit that she'd left the children alone while she collected her benefit. Andrews calls Social Services to deal with the children, and Steeds warns Kirby that she could be prosecuted for being unregistered and for leaving the children alone. The officers go to Jones who says he's sorted everything out and proudly waves Kirby's IOU under their noses. They arrest him for demanding money with menaces.

This is still only bare bones (we don't yet have interesting characters, for a start), but it does fulfil the requirements of a plot, because it tells us why these things have happened. It also has some unexpected benefits because our sympathies are constantly shifting from one character to another. We might think that both have some justification for what they do and for feeling in the end that they have been treated unfairly. There is plenty of opportunity for them to grow.

EXERCISE

The aims of this exercise are for pupils to:

- learn to ask the questions that will lead to the development of plot

- select and develop the dramatic potential in a story.

The following newspaper story contains enough material for a whole play.

Distribute copies of the story to the class. Ask them to read it carefully and then break down the narrative into its principal events: first this happened; then this; then this. The task is simplified because the reporter, Alex Starmer, has already done much of the work by giving us the specific times of the events. The important thing is that pupils concentrate on what happened, not on why.

The next stage is to re-write these principal events and include the cause for each. In other words, pupils should try to say why this thing happened and, in doing so, develop the story into a plot.

Deaf gunman snapped over late Giro

Alex Starmer

ELEVEN DAYS ago, David Stone signed on at his local Unemployment Benefit Office, after fighting as a mercenary in Bosnia. He expected to get his Giro cheque within a few days, but it got lost in the post and he was told he might have to wait 13 weeks to receive payment.

Last Friday, Stone left his flat in Hornsey, north London, and made his way to nearby Highgate.

At 11.50am, armed with a revolver, he held up Barclays Bank in Highgate High Street and escaped with £1,600 in cash.

By 12.10pm, after a chase during which he hijacked a council dustcart, Stone was dead, shot through the forehead by a police marksman.

To the press, he immediately became the 'dustcart gunman', a robber who told road sweepers, as he took their vehicle: 'A man's gotta do what a man's gotta do', and who shot at police cars as he drive down Highgate Hill to Holloway where he abandoned the cart.

Police used a helicopter and 13 patrol cars in the chase, which ended in a timber yard. One witness said that in the timber yard there was a stand-off for a second, then a massive exchange of gunfire.

What nobody in the bank, during the chase, or at the scene of Stone's death knew was that, according to his girl-friend, he was completely deaf and would not have heard warnings shouted at him.

'He saw his doctor and he was going to get a hearing aid fitted,' his friend, Connie Smith, said last night. 'He was good at lip reading but that's all he could do. I reckon it must have been all the bombs and things that made him deaf over the years.

'It's like the police have a shoot-to-kill policy, but they could have just wounded him instead of killing him. They could have shot him in the arm or something, not in the forehead.'

Stone joined the Navy when he was 16. He moved on to the Marines and the Special Boat Squadron, before serving for six years in the French Foreign Legion.

When the war broke out in Bosnia, Stone went there and spent the last two years fighting as a mercenary for the Muslims, travelling between Sarajevo and the flat in Hornsey where he helped to nurse Ms Smith, who has cancer.

'He used to say to me, when he got back from Bosnia, that I wouldn't believe the things Serbs did to the women and children,' she said last night. 'He always talked about how awful it was that the poorest people would be shot queuing for black bread. Just the other week he said he wanted to go to Mogadishu. He said, "I'll bring a couple of orphans back".

'He wasn't interested in money at all. If you needed some money, he would take the last few pounds out of his pocket and give it to you. Everyone liked him and he had never been in trouble before in his life … I think he was a victim of circumstances. His brain was just mixed up.'

'He liked the army life,' another friend said yesterday. 'He just couldn't settle down to civilian life. He was desperately looking for work and the Giro thing was the straw that broke the camel's back.'

At 12.30pm on Friday, 40 minutes after David Stone walked into the bank and 20 minutes after he was killed, the midday post arrived at his flat. A Giro cheque for £86 dropped through the letterbox.

The Observer,
17th October 1993

Next, ask the class to try and identify the dramatic moment(s) in the story:

- the soldier's experiences in Bosnia;

- his return to England;

- his being told he must wait thirteen weeks for giro;

- the bank raid;

- the hijacking of the dustcart;

- the shooting.

Discuss with the class the sort of emotions they would want to stir in an audience if they were writing this script. Would they want the audience to be interested, for example, in:

- the drama of the crime?

- the shoot-out in Holloway Road?

- the reactions of his girlfriend?

Would they, alternatively, want to arouse more complex emotions? This story is rich in pathos, dark humour and irony; the giro dropping through the letter-box twenty minutes after the man's death is the sort of detail few dramatists would dare invent.

Finally, you could ask the class to reflect on the pause before the shooting. This moment, when nothing happens, might nevertheless be the moment of greatest drama in the story.

Follow-up suggestions

1. Pupils with course work due are in a similar position to a writer commissioned to write something to a deadline. They can't afford to sit around waiting for a story to drop into their lap: they have to make their stories happen. One way of speeding up the creative process is by careful research.

Suggest to the class that they find some sort of occupation which interests them and to which they have some access; perhaps through family or friends. Ask them to find out as much as they can about the sort of people who do that job:

- what time they start work;

- what the job involves;

- how they speak to one another;

- what they eat for lunch;

- where they socialise:

- in short, as much as they can about their working lives.

They should then sift through this information to find that fragment which might become a story. They may not have something which could be used intact, but they will have anecdotes, bits of stories, characters that they can build on. The skill lies in knowing the fragment when it appears and then in asking, why?

2.   An alternative to the above activity (or an extension of it) is to adapt an already existing story. Decisions about what to retain and what to leave out will force pupils to identify the dramatically important moments of the narrative. Description will have to be sketched in through stage directions and characters revealed entirely through what they do, what they say about themselves, and what others say about them.

Some stories lend themselves to this approach more readily than others. John Steinbeck's novel *Of Mice and Men*, for example, is already written very like a script: each chapter reads like a separate scene and the dialogue is stark, powerful.

4. MAKING US CARE – AN EXERCISE IN CREATING CHARACTER

Plays are about people. A playwright may want to write about pollution or poverty or ambition; she may have some original and weighty things to say about life, the universe and everything. But if she wants us to listen to what she has to say, she must embody those ideas in people that we, the audience, will care about.

This is not to say that we must like or approve of those characters but that we must be sufficiently interested in them to want to know why they do the things they do and what will happen to them. Their fate must affect us in some way.

The writers and producers of all successful soap operas understand and exploit this basic fact. We turn on in our millions week after week not because we are interested in theories of love, greed, crime or punishment but simply because we want to know what is going to happen to the characters: we care about them.

What is a character?

The human imagination has been 'colonised' to its remotest regions by the inventions of storytellers. Our heads are full of people who have never existed, and yet we seldom stop to ask a very obvious question: what exactly is a character?

Character is a word with a complex history of meaning and association. Often it appears to be synonymous with 'person', with all that word's connotations of wholeness. In Greek, however, character meant an instrument for making a distinctive mark; it then became the mark itself before being used to denote an essential quality and, much later, an odd or eccentric person. If we return for a moment to the early sense of character as a distinctive feature rather than a whole individual this may help to make the creation of characters in fiction a little clearer.

Characters in plays and novels are not real and they are not whole. They have no future and no past; no parents and no relatives; they do not dream or desire. They are features, traits – what the French philosopher Roland Barthes calls 'flickers of meaning'.

Taken together, these flickers merely *suggest* the complexity of a real human being. This is not to denigrate those writers whose skill convinces us that what we are seeing is real: what characters in plays and novels say and do can affect us deeply. It is to understand, more fully, the true nature of that skill.

The way in which books and plays are studied in schools encourages us to talk about characters from fiction as if they were real flesh and blood, people with a life independent of the work of fiction. Indeed, we are often encouraged to measure the success of a fiction by the 'authenticity' or 'realism' of the characters. But to treat such inventions as real when we know they are not may cause us to make fundamental mistakes about the nature of fiction and to misunderstand the conventions governing it.

Let me give an example of a 'flicker of meaning', taken from real life. A couple of weeks ago I was talking to an elderly man. He began telling me about the state of his marriage, his second. It was a thoroughly bad arrangement: his wife was 'impossible, totally unco-operative'. He had, he explained, been, 'looking for second happiness. I could've found it … I travel by bus quite a bit. There's a woman I used to see … moved to Horsham from Fareham. She'd do me fine. I know where she lives, but I haven't been on the bus lately.'

This is one of Roland Barthes's 'flickers'. For me at least, a vivid character flickers for a moment in front of my eyes at the pause between 'I could've found it' and 'I travel by bus quite a bit'. This little speech has the brilliant unexpectedness of real talk. You can, if you are clever enough, invent this kind of thing but you can also stumble across it. You need only listen.

The arrival of an enigma

Any characters that have emerged from the previous exercises in this book have been stumbled on by chance rather than created deliberately. They may have grown out of the exercises in writing dialogue, possibly without any real sense of purpose or control.

This kind of creation (haphazard though it may seem) is, in its randomness, similar to the way in which we get to know people in daily life. We overhear a snatch of conversation; we learn of an occupation or ambition; we discern a tone of voice, a manner; we guess and we predict.

However, many people want something less chaotic and more ordered: they want a clear idea of their characters before they start to write. There might appear to be a logic to this approach, but it allows no room for contingency: it doesn't give the characters a chance to grow and change as the plot unfolds. It's rather like demanding to read someone's autobiography before meeting him.

Inherent in this approach is a fundamental confusion about how characters are created and what their relationship to events is, a confusion displayed in the old examination question: 'Does character create plot or does plot create character?' The answer, of course, is 'yes' to both parts of the question. The kind of person we are determines our behaviour, and what happens to us influences our character. We cannot separate who we are from what we do. In plays, likewise, the characters are what carries the action of the play forward. They make things happen and they must grow and develop along with the plot.

If we change one character in a play by making her tell a lie, we will have to change the plot because her lie will affect what happens; alter the plot by having something terrible happen to a character, and we will have to rethink the character because he's not going to be the same person afterwards.

Rather than seeing this as a limitation we should welcome it as one of the chief joys of writing. There is no need to write a life history for every character, no need to know what she had for breakfast or what GCSEs he got. Characters can, indeed must, be fluid; they must change and develop and be as enigmatic and as unpredictable as real, flesh and blood people. They must, in other words, be people about whom we can care.

EXERCISE

The aim of this exercise is:

- to use a process of interrogation to help pupils acquire their first glimpse of a character.

- to create a character from nothing or

- to develop an already existing character.

Ask pupils to think of someone they have seen more than once but don't know; someone seen on the way to school perhaps, or noticed from a bus.

Alternatively, they might use a character who already exists in a sketchy form in their story.

Ask them to give the following information about this person (the right-hand column list examples of this information):

Information	Example
Three short statements of fact about this person.	– He wears a grey overcoat summer and winter. – His shoes are always polished. – He nods to me but never speaks.
A sound which they associate with the person.	– Leather shoes crunching on a gravel path.
A possession.	– A medal for bravery.
A season they associate with the person.	– Spring.
An item of furniture.	– A straight-backed wooden chair.
A smell.	– Hand-rolled cigarettes.
The person's ambition.	– To keep out of the way.
A time of day.	– Early morning.
A colour.	– Silver.
A recurring dream.	– A library with no books.
A fear.	– Blindness.
A word.	– Honesty.
Something the person says.	'It's all a waste of time.'

(Pupils will have to invent many of the answers to these questions.)

The important thing here is the line of speech. Some of the other information might be useful as stage directions or notes for an actor, but, as far as the writer is concerned, it's what the character says that matters. Pupils should now try to build on this line of speech, perhaps by working it into a monologue.

Hot-seating

Hot-seating represents another way of organising this method of interrogation of a character. Pupils should work with a partner, taking it in turns to be put in the 'hot seat' and interviewed.

The questions should begin simply, e.g.:

> 'How old are you?'
> 'What colour is your hair?'
> 'What is your name?'

They should gradually become more probing:

> 'What is your favourite book?'
> 'Describe your recurring dream.'

The idea is that through sensitive and prolonged questioning you can begin to elicit a character. It's amazing how easy the technique is to learn and how quickly pupils will begin to inhabit their creation.

Try to get individuals to identify the point at which their character began to be real to them. If they can say which questions were most useful in this respect they might get some idea of what sort of things they need to ask themselves when they are writing a character.

One way of extending this exercise, in a written form, is for pupils to write a postcard, diary entry or shopping list (other forms are possible – all that's important is that the piece should not be too self-consciously crafted) for the character on whom they are working.

Stereotypes

If teachers want to stop pupils writing, or thinking, about character, all they have to do is to suggest that what they have created is a stereotype. This term is now frequently (and lazily) used to denote not simply a lack of originality in a character, but disapproval. The problem with this usage is that it is plain unhelpful. 'Stereotype' becomes one of those words which merely stop us examining what is going on, stop all conversation, all debate, all thought.

If, as teachers, we are tempted to dismiss a character as a stereotype, we should ask ourselves whether the remark is meant to be helpful ('I've seen plenty of characters like this before, and her behaviour is entirely predictable') or unhelpful ('I disapprove of this person you've invented; he says and does things I don't like, and I don't want to know about him.').

In many ways, we should be encouraging pupils to write things of which other people won't approve. If people are upset by what pupils write, the chances are they've made something powerful, perhaps even something original. They should only start worrying if their characters are stereotypical in the sense of being obvious: writers should always be looking for the unexpected.

Follow-up suggestions

1.   Show the class a short extract from a popular soap opera (or another programme which is attempting to be realistic in its depiction of characters) and another from a programme like *Star Trek* (or another programme which has a 'cartoon' quality to its characterisation).

Ask the class to identify the 'goodies' and the 'baddies' in each and encourage them to be specific about how they can tell which is which: by appearance, speech or action?

Pupils will probably find it easier to say which character is the 'goody' and which the 'baddy' in a science fiction programme like *Star Trek*, because right and wrong are signalled clearly to the audience in this kind of film. Soap operas may give indications of which character deserves our approval or our censure, but they are usually less clear cut; their characters are fuller, and we see more sides to them. In great drama, this is even more true, and it is for this sort of richness and complexity of character that we should be aiming.

2.   Now ask the class to examine their response to characters in both genres and to say which most engage their emotions. Ask them to be specific about what they feel and why they feel it. Did *Star Trek* ever make anyone cry? How does one get hooked on a soap?

Such a discussion is likely to reveal that the soap evokes more profound emotions than whole armies of Klingons pillaging The Starship Enterprise. Even the softest soap opera deals with drama which arises not from a simple struggle between good and bad but from the interplay of characters who are, like all of us, a little bit of both. Drama, we are often told, consists in conflict; characters who embody contradictory impulses are always in conflict with themselves – that is what makes them interesting.

A dramatist must examine the actions and motivation of even the most reprehensible characters and present them to us as people with whom we can connect. This means that we, the audience, must 'care' as much about the rapist as about his victim; the torturer as her prey. We may, finally, be invited to make a judgement, but before we can do that we must understand. This is an uncomfortable but fundamental truth of all good drama.

This is not the sort of thing some people want to hear. They want their drama in black and white, with all the issues clear cut, to be able to condemn without needing to understand. They don't want the messy complexity of life, which is where drama thrives; they want their playwrights to become preachers and their plays to become propaganda.

But it is not the job of the playwright to tell the audience what to think. It is the job of the playwright to make them think. The best drama grows in that grey moral area where we are not sure who is 'right' and who is 'wrong'. George Bernard Shaw pointed out that in a good play everyone is right, and one definition of drama might be the clash of right and right or, even, of wrong and wrong. If you want to see this happening to devastating effect, look at Ariel Dorfman's play *Death and the Maiden,* in which torturer and victim appear to meet face to face.

5. MONOLOGUES INTO DIALOGUES

Tom Stoppard says that writing a play is a good way of having an argument with yourself. This is a good description of what it feels like to sit down with your characters and try to make them speak. However, it is not at all easy to keep two or more people in your head at one time, and a good starting-point is the monologue, a form which until recently has been largely neglected.

EXERCISE

The aim of this exercise is:

- to help pupils reach the point where they can handle the complexity of having two or more characters interacting with one another.

The exercise explores the development and revelation of character through monologues, written individually, and then moves gradually into a collaborative exercise designed to end in a short play.

Session One

Ask the group to consider a situation in which two people meet after a long period of separation. The meeting must involve each character in a journey which may be as short as a few minutes or as long as several days.

Discuss various possibilities and encourage them to think of dramatically productive situations: the child, adopted years before, meeting her natural parent; the husband visiting a wife in prison; the childhood sweethearts, separated by fate, meeting towards the end of their lives.

Ask pupils to work in pairs to agree on the bare outline of events: who is meeting whom, where and why?

Now ask pupils, on their own, to write a monologue in four paragraphs (each of which should be no more than about ten or twelve sentences in length) in which they describe their thoughts and emotions in each situation. The four parts are as follows:

1. The journey

2. The meeting

3. The return

4. The epilogue

(They are to imagine this final paragraph to have been written some time after the event, as a kind of summing up of what the characters learned from the experience.)

Finally, in order to build an element of conflict into the situation, secretly tell one half of the pairs that they have been longing for this meeting and the other half that they are dreading it.

Session Two

When pupils have completed their monologues and are working in pairs, ask them to read their finished piece to their partner. There will be details which they will need to tidy up: tenses which should agree; places; names, etc.

This is a good point at which to hear some of the results presented to the rest of the class. As always, the important thing is to listen and not try to impose an outcome.

Next, ask pupils to read their monologues again, this time 'dovetailing' the paragraphs, so that A reads her first paragraph followed by B's, then A's second and so on. Once again, listen carefully to the results.

What is likely to happen is that the monologues will begin to 'speak' to one another. We will be hearing only the thoughts of the characters and not actual speech, but the feeling of two people communicating different responses to the same event will emerge. The resulting conflict of attitudes is the beginning of drama.

Read the monologues again, this time alternating them sentence by sentence so that we begin to edge towards something that has the feel of dialogue. Discuss the effects that become apparent: could any part of this be converted easily into real dialogue? What problems would arise if we wanted, through dialogue, to communicate to an audience the different attitudes of the characters to each other?

Ask pupils, in pairs, to turn the second part of their monologues (i.e. the meeting itself) into a dialogue. This part of the exercise, potentially the most difficult but also the most rewarding, might best be approached by asking the simple question, 'What did you say to one another?'

Arriving at a mutual version will require a certain measure of negotiation, and some agreement about what actually took place will have to be reached. The important thing is not to lose sight of the fact that the audience doesn't want to see a simple conflict between right and wrong but to understand what is happening to these two people. The aim is to get the energy of dialogue while retaining the subtlety of monologue.

Stretching the exercise to its limit, try converting both monologues into a short play by adding new material and perhaps introducing new characters. The principal characters might need someone to talk to on the journey, or someone to confide in afterwards.

At this stage, pupils will need to consider not only characterisation and motivation (the key ingredients of the monologues) but also the movement and maintenance of a narrative. The first step will be to decide exactly what this story is about and begin to structure a plot.

The following examples, written by sixth-form students, demonstrates the process of this exercise.

The Journey
1 How will you look, John?
2 How will you feel towards me after how long has it been now?
3 Funny what can happen, eh?
4 Only two years ago we were both line managers.
5 Now I'm regional manager and you're ...?
6 Well it doesn't matter, anyway.
7 Talking to myself.
8 Must be anxious or something.
9 Seeing John again after – what did I say? – three years?
10 Sure to be pleased.

The Meeting
1 Happydale Day Care and Recuperation Centre.
2 Hmm. No stairs, just a ... a wheelchair ramp.
3 I saw you as I strode down that long hall glancing at those sad eyes and drawn faces.
4 You never let your gaze leave me.
5 At first I couldn't believe it was you.
6 You seemed so much smaller, so insignificant.
7 Only your eyes were alive as I approached you.

8 You wouldn't talk to me about the old times.
9 I couldn't just let you sit there.
10 Then you swivelled right round in your wheelchair and you shouted . . . .
11 'Get out!'

The Return
1 I ran to the car and locked myself in.
2 How did it happen to you?
3 How could you have grown so old?
4 I sat and shivered in the car, John, and then I drove.
5 I drove to the top of Newbury Cliff.
6 I hurled alcohol and soul into the sea.
7 I made this recording.
8 I told this cold microphone what I could never say to your face.
9 I said, 'Sorry.'

Postscript
At least he's being well looked after.

Matthew Foster

The Journey
1 How did he find me?
2 Two years, two years away from him and his innocent eyes and smug grin.
3 It's bad enough being trapped here and forced to spend every day with a bunch of fools.
4 Now the man who caused me so much pain is coming to visit.
5 He looked away for a moment and that was my life over.
6 Spinal cord broken beyond repair because of him.
7 'Not guilty of negligence', but what could they know?
8 And just as if my life wasn't bad enough, he tracks me down.
9 Phones and tells me he's coming to visit.
10 Twenty feet down that corridor to meet the man who ruined my life.

The Meeting
1 It was awful, having to look at him.
2 Before the accident I had a good six inches on him.
3 Now he can peer down his nose like I'm some kind of insect.
4 At least I got it all off my chest.
5 All the rage that had built up over the years.
6 God, it felt good.
7 I watched him as he stood there, listening to me tell him every painful detail.

8 The loss of independence.
9 The humiliation.
10 The anger.
11 I let him know just what he had done to me.

The Return
1 The silence that has settled on the Day Centre is chilling.
2 Everywhere seems empty.
3 Everyone else is shunning me because of what I said.
4 I feel empty inside myself.
5 He left with his guilt.
6 Now I have nothing.
7 It was only the anger that kept me going.
8 Now that's gone ...
9 ... what can I do?

Postscript
Why did I set free the rage that kept me alive?

Chris Wallace

This is how Chris and Matthew's Monologues work when they are combined line by line:

The Journey
1 How will you look, John?
1 How did he find me?
2 How will you feel towards me after how long has it been now?
2 Two years, two years away from him and his innocent eyes and smug grin.
3 Funny what can happen, eh?
3 It's bad enough being trapped here forced to spend every day with a bunch of fools.
4 Only two years ago we were both line managers.
4 Now the man who caused me so much pain is coming to visit.
5 Now I'm regional manager and you're ... ?
5 He looked away for a moment and that was my life over.
6 Well it doesn't matter, anyway.
6 Spinal cord broken beyond repair because of him.
7 Talking to myself.
7 'Not guilty of negligence', but what could they know?
8 Must be anxious or something.
8 And just as if my life wasn't bad enough, he tracks me down.
9 Seeing John again after – what did I say? – three years?

9 Phones and tells me he's coming to visit.
10 Sure to be pleased.
10 Twenty feet down that corridor to meet the man who ruined my life.

The Meeting

1 Happydale Day Care and Recuperation Centre.
1 It was awful, having to look at him.
2 Hmm. No stairs, just a . . . a wheelchair ramp.
2 Before the accident I had a good six inches on him.
3 I saw you as I strode down that long hall glancing at those sad eyes and drawn faces.
3 Now he can peer down my nose like I'm some sort of insect.
4 You never let your gaze leave me.
4 At least I got it all off my chest.
5 At first I couldn't beleive it was you.
5 All the rage that had built up over the years.
6 You seemed so much smaller, so insignificant.
6 God, it felt good.
7 Only your eyes were alive as I approached you.
7 I watched him as he stood there, listening to me tell him every painful detail.
8 You wouldn't talk to me about the old times.
8 The loss of independence.
9 I couldn't just let you sit there.
9 The humiliation.
10 Then you swivelled right round in your wheelchair and you shouted. . . .
10 The anger.
11 I let him know what he had done to me.
11 'Get out!'

The return

1 I ran to the car and locked myself in.
1 The silence that has settled on the Day Centre is chilling.
2 How did it happen to you?
2 Everywhere seems empty.
3 How could you have grown so old?
3 Everyone else is shunning me because of what I said.
4 I sat and shivered in the car, John, and then I drove.
4 I feel empty inside myself.
5 I drove to the top of Newbury Cliff.
5 He left with his guilt.
6 I hurled alcohol and soul into the sea.

6 Now I have nothing.

7 I made this recording.

7 It was only the anger that kept me going.

8 I told this cold microphone what I could

8 Now that's gone …

9 I said, 'Sorry.'

9 … what can I do?

Postscript

Why did I set free the rage that kept me alive?

At least he's well looked after.

This might be a good point at which to remind pupils that in real life people seldom say exactly what they think. The person who is blisteringly honest about everything all the time does not exist; and if he did, we might be tempted to ask, 'What exactly is he hiding?' We all disguise our true feelings most of the time: the dramatist, however, has to know something about the 'secret' life of her characters and the subtext of what they are saying.

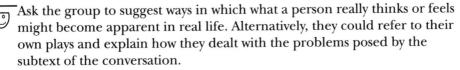 Ask the group to suggest ways in which what a person really thinks or feels might become apparent in real life. Alternatively, they could refer to their own plays and explain how they dealt with the problems posed by the subtext of the conversation.

Follow-up suggestions

1.   There is no reason why the first part of this exercise might not become an end in itself, the four parts of the monologue forming the basis for one self-contained piece in which we view a situation through the eyes of one person.

2.   Alternatively, the first part of the exercise could be turned into a solo piece of work in which each pupil becomes responsible for both characters.

Clearly the most important thing is to devise a situation in which there is a potential conflict between the two characters. This need not mean that they argue or fight – it could be that a doctor has bad news which she has to break to someone expecting good news. Alternatively, one character might wish to conceal something important from the other, as in an interview with police.

There has lately been something of a revival of interest in the monologue, both on television and radio. In the hands of a writer like Alan Bennett, the monologue is a form capable of great subtlety, and although (as Bennett says about his creations) 'none of these narrators after all is telling the whole story', we do not miss the interventions of other characters when we watch something like *Bed Among the Lentils*. We may have only Susan's view of the world, but by the end of the 'play' we feel we know her perhaps better than if she had been one character among many in a conventional play. In these monologues, the characters reveal themselves to us in a way which is wholly convincing. One of the reasons for this is because, whatever they appear to be doing, the characters are not talking to themselves but to one other character who is always there with them: the camera.

6. DRAMATIC STRUCTURE

Most dramatists, certainly those working in television, will write nothing until they have a clear plot and a well-articulated dramatic structure. Making even half an hour of television is very expensive, and producers are not going to dish out money if they don't think the play will work.

The requirement to plan properly may be turned to advantage. Once we have the plan (what television writers call the 'treatment'), we can concentrate on developing character, secure in the knowledge that our story will work. Most writers would say that the treatment is more important than the actual writing of the dialogue: it is certainly the most difficult part of making the play. We might start with a character or an incident or even an emotion that we want to write about, but without the treatment we will have no idea of the dramatic significance of the character or incident and no idea how the emotion can be conveyed in dramatic terms.

A useful class discussion could centre on the differences between watching a play and reading a novel. We choose a book and spend hours or weeks reading it, skip passages or whole pages we don't like, re-read bits that we like or that don't make sense – we may even, if we wish, read the end first to find out what happens. In short, we can deal with a novel in our own way and in our own time. A play in performance, on the other hand, exists only for a brief period of time, and then it's gone. We only get one go at it, and, if it doesn't hold us there and then, we can walk out of the theatre or switch off the TV. With so many channels available on television this is an acute problem for writers, producers and directors and can lead to a concentration on the sensational at the expense of the truly dramatic. The fact remains that the play must hold the attention of the audience or they will not attend. In this respect, television drama is no different from the theatre of Shakespeare or Aeschylus.

Building the play

The following exercise uses the plot of Henrik Ibsen's *An Enemy of the People* to demonstrate the importance of dramatic structure. The play, set in a town in southern Norway, deals with, among other things, a problem familiar to all of us today: pollution.[*] If you are not familiar with the play, it is important that you (but not your pupils) know the plot, viz.:

> Dr Stockman is the Medical Officer of the town's new medicinal baths. His brother Peter, the town's Mayor and Chief of Police, is the Governor of the baths and the inspiration behind the project. He hopes that his scheme will bring visitors and financial prosperity to the town.
>
> Dr Stockman, however, has discovered that the water which supplies the baths is polluted and poses a serious threat to public health. He is thus in a position to save the town from disaster. Unfortunately, no one wants to hear what he has to say, because the prosperity of the town depends on the success of the scheme.
>
> Dr Stockman struggles against the prejudice of his brother, the local press and even the ordinary townspeople in order to save them from disaster. The play ends with Stockman and his family completely isolated from the community and Stockman himself labelled 'An Enemy of the People'.

The issues raised by the play are complex: the pollution seems to be coming from the local tannery owned by Morten Kill. Morten is Dr Stockman's wife's foster-father and a public benefactor.

Dr Stockman himself is an arrogant man who seems to enjoy his lone struggle against ignorance and prejudice, and we are never quite sure of his motives for taking his stand. Is he really the disinterested doctor with only the health and well-being of the people at heart? Or is he allowing his vanity and pride to influence his actions?

It is likely that Ibsen deliberately built these cross-currents into his play in order to bring out all these complexities of the situation. Every possible point of view is represented by someone, and everyone has an interest in the issues: everyone is 'right'.

---

*Other plays could be used just as easily: the process involves writing a short description of each scene (in the form of a 'headline') on an index card, e.g.: 'In which Penny finds her uncle's will', 'In which Martin calls Michael a coward', etc. and then spreading the cards out on the floor and experimenting with the structure by arranging them in various ways, moving scenes about, until you get the effect you want.

EXERCISE

For this exercise, the plot of a new play, based on *An Enemy of the People,* has been broken down into major scenes and a brief outline of each written on a card. The cards also give brief notes on characters, situation and the basic elements of the scene, e.g. 'Two months before the start of the holiday season a doctor in a small seaside town has discovered that the sea water is polluted. His brother is the mayor. What does he do?'

The important thing is that each card gives the same very basic information (a seaside town dependent on tourism, etc.) but no indication of the overall plot of the play. The idea is that each group should concentrate only on the detail of their particular scene without being concerned with what happens before or after.

Divide the class into groups of two, three or four. Put them somewhere where they can work separately and give each group one of the cards. Each group should write the scene using the information given. Some groups may request further clarification, but you should try to keep this to a minimum and in no circumstances give away the rest of the plot.

Scene: A small flat in a large city

An elderly couple

The couple are planning their summer holiday. They always go to the same small, quiet seaside town where the beaches are noted for their cleanliness. They have very little money.

Scene: A local government office

Council executive and tourist officer

A small seaside town, dependent on tourism, is to be awarded a 'blue flag' for its clean beaches. The chief executive of the council has just been told of lethal pollution in the sea water. It is March, and the tourist season is one month away.

Scene: A local government office

Mayor and tourist officer

This small seaside town, dependent on tourism, is to be awarded a 'blue flag' for its clean beaches. The mayor wants to make the most of the news.

Scene: A middle-class house in a seaside town

A doctor and the doctor's wife/husband

In a small seaside town, famous for its clean beaches and natural beauty and dependent on tourism, the doctor has discovered lethal pollution of the sea water. He has told the authorities, and now an angry mob of the town's people have besieged the house.

Scene: A pub in a small seaside town

Two unemployed hotel staff

A small seaside town with high unemployment and only seasonal trade is dependent on tourism. A pollution scare started by the town's doctor has caused the collapse of the holiday trade and thrown these two people out of work. They are plotting revenge on the doctor.

Scene: A newspaper office

Editor and town doctor

A small seaside town, dependent on tourism, is to be awarded a 'blue flag' for its clean beaches. The doctor has found lethal pollution of the sea water. He wants the newspaper to run the story. It is March, and the tourist season is one month away.

Scene: A middle-class house in a seaside town

A doctor and the doctor's wife/husband

In a small seaside town, famous for its clean beaches and natural beauty and dependent on tourism, the doctor has discovered lethal contamination in the sea water. What should he/she do?

Scene: A council office

Doctor and Chief Executive of Council

A small seaside town, dependent on tourism, is to be awarded a 'blue flag' for its clean beaches. Trade is seasonal, and there is high unemployment. The doctor has found the sea water is lethally polluted. The tourist season is one month away. The doctor wants the council to close the beaches and warn the public.

Scene: A small seaside hotel

The owner and husband/wife

The couple who own this hotel have invested their life savings in it. The holiday season is one month away, and they are preparing for what they hope will be a good year. Last season was a disaster.

Scene: A street in a small seaside town

The town doctor and a local hotel keeper

A small seaside town, dependent on tourism, is to be awarded a 'blue flag' for its clean beaches. Trade is seasonal, and the hotel owner's life savings are at risk. The doctor has found the sea water to be lethally polluted. The tourist season is one month away.

Scene: An office

Chief Executive of Council and Newspaper Editor

A small seaside town, dependent on tourism, is to be awarded a 'blue flag' for its clean beaches. Trade is seasonal, and there is high unemployment. The local doctor has found the sea water to be lethally polluted. The tourist season is one month away.

The doctor wants the council to close the beaches and warn the public. The council executive and the newspaper editor are determined to keep it secret.

Once the groups have written their scenes, you will need to have a note of which group has worked on which scene. I make a simple plan of the room, mark the position of each group and allocate a number to each.

The next task is to 'conduct' the class in a reading of the finished scenes so that a complete narrative gradually emerges. At this stage, a straightforward, 'linear' read-through is advisable, starting with the discovery of the contamination and working through to the scene in which the doctor is besieged by the mob. It is important that each group knows when to read their scene.

At this stage it is also best to say nothing about the effectiveness of the individual scenes themselves or how they fit together. The important thing is that the story be allowed to unfold. It is the revelation of the narrative which is important – seeing how one's own scene fits in with everyone else's contribution. The aim should be to put the events into a logical sequence.

Now ask the class to consider what sort of 'play' has emerged from the exercise:

- How clear, or confused, is the story?

- What kind of story is it?

- How well has it been told?

Next, experiment with the structure of the 'play' by rearranging the scenes and then reading them in a new order. For example, what would happen if the final scene came first, so that we saw the doctor and his family besieged in their house at the very beginning of the play and only then saw the discovery of the pollution?

This would involve telling the story in flashback, a technique used extensively in film and TV. In flashback, the story is told in reverse. Encourage the class to discuss what difference this makes. Is the story still the same? How would an audience react to the change?

Flashback forces the audience to watch with a different kind of attention. Perhaps they will observe the characters and their motives more closely if they're not worrying about what happens next. They might become even more interested in how a decent, public-spirited doctor could get to the point where his neighbours want to kill him.

Take, as another example, the scene in which the old couple are planning their holiday. If we place it before the doctor discovers the pollution the result is *pathos*: the discovery makes us feel sorry for them. 'How miserable,' we say, 'to have planned a holiday in a place like that.'

Now place the same scene after the discovery, and the audience will know something which the characters don't know. The audience will see the couple discussing the cost, making plans, looking forward to a holiday which will end in disaster. 'Don't do it!' they'll cry. 'Go to Mallorca instead!' Allowing the audience to know something which the characters don't know is an extremely useful device and is used to achieve one of the most powerful of dramatic effects, *irony*.

It is worth spending some time examining the impact of such apparently small changes to the running order of the play so that the importance of the structure becomes clear. It is also worth considering whether or not characters need to be rewritten in the light of such changes.

For example, if we decide to go for an ironic effect by introducing our elderly couple after the doctor's discovery, we might want to play down the sentimentality of the situation by making the couple 'tougher': less like pathetic victims and more like people with choices.

Any one of dozens of changes to the running order of our play is possible, and each change will produce a different effect or shift the emphasis in some way.

Follow-up suggestions

1.   A similar exercise may be done with any 'well made' play with a strong narrative drive. However, it is worth experimenting with a more impressionistic form, like Dylan Thomas's *Under Milk Wood*, which achieves its effect through the gradual accumulation of fragmented and unrelated scenes.

The following suggestion uses scenes relating to a vague and unspecified war. Each scene should be written by a different individual or pair, with no other knowledge or information, before being orchestrated into a whole by the teacher.

- Two old soldiers discuss the benefits of regular wars.

- Two children are caught stealing food for their starving family.

- A woman whose son has been struck dumb by the horror of war tells her story to a stranger.

- A council workman arrives to pull down a war memorial, but is stopped by the son/daughter of one of the men it names.

- A mother tries to stop her son becoming a soldier.

- A poor man arrives home with the boots he has taken from a dead soldier.

- A farmer and his wife plead with soldiers about to take their crops and animals.

- The curator of a museum describes entering the building after it has been looted.

- Two isolated soldiers discuss what to do with a troublesome prisoner.

- Two politicians write a speech in which they try to make heavy losses sound like a victory for their side.

- A soldier asks his enemy to hide him.

- A priest preaches to soldiers before a battle.

- A priest preaches to soldiers after a battle.

- Parents ask an official for news of their missing child.

- A woman tries to sell her wedding ring to buy food for her child.

- An old man on his death-bed remembers, as a young man, killing an enemy.

- A teacher visits the battlefield with her class fifty years later.

.e exciting thing about this approach is that there is no right way to
resent the piece and therefore the possible permutations are far greater.
Any change in running order will produce a different effect and the effect
of any scene will alter depending on where it appears.

What would happen, for example, if the scene in which the council workers
pull down the war memorial appears after the scene in which politicians try
to make heavy losses appear like a victory? What would be the effect of
placing the scene in which a mother tries to stop her son enlisting after we
have seen a poor man with the boots he has taken from a dead soldier? How
would we feel about those starving children stealing food if they appeared
before the teacher visits the battlefield with her class?

Finally, ask each student to choose the single most evocative or important
line in their scene and simply read around the class.

The following example was produced by students at Bewdley High School in
Worcestershire.

EMMA: War keeps the population down.

KATE: We took what wasn't ours.

ROBIN: He must have seen something awful.

HELEN: Do you want everyone to forget what happened?

CLAIRE: It'll be fun! Fun!

RUTH: They would have just gone to waste.

IAN: We'll starve … we'll starve.

FAYE: I spent the whole of my life.

ROBIN: Put him below … below.

CLAIRE: I'm not the enemy; your gun is.

LUCY: You are fighting for your country … your beliefs.

HOLLY: Stick together and we shall win.

WILL: It's all very complicated, sir.

JO: I wouldn't sell it unless I was really desperate.

CAROL: All I had to do was pick up a gun and kill.

JO: Over there, where the poppies are coming through, was the school.

When the students were working on this particular text, a powerful and haunting effect was achieved simply by having Will's 'It's all very complicated, sir' repeated several times during the reading.

Postscript

I live on the West coast of Wales. One day the local water company told the hotel keepers in a small seaside town a few miles away that there was a problem with the water supply and that they should boil all water before using it. No one else was given this advice, even though it was in the middle of the holiday season and the population of the town was more than double what it is in winter.

Some friends who run a shop were told about the water board's advice by their next-door neighbour, who happens to run a hotel. Being public-spirited, they promptly put a notice in their shop window warning holidaymakers to boil their water before drinking it. Why, they asked, should only people staying in hotels know about the risk?
Within minutes of putting the notice up, they had a visit from another, furious shopkeeper demanding that they take it down. His reason? If tourists found out that the water wasn't safe to drink they would go somewhere else and trade would suffer. Incredible as it may seem, the man demanding the removal of the notice was the local chemist. I'm glad to say my friends stood their ground and refused.

The similarities to Ibsen's story are obvious. Indeed *An Enemy of the People* has striking similarities to several other stories, most notably Steven Spielberg's film *Jaws*, in which the hero has to fight the prejudice of the townspeople for the sake of the safety of innocent holidaymakers. Good stories get recycled.

7. THE SCENE

A twenty-five minute TV drama may have anything between twenty and forty scenes: a stage play lasting two hours may have only three or four. What, if anything, do the two forms have in common? Here are two areas of overlap:

–   A scene is a subdivision of a play, its basic 'building block'. On stage and on television, the scene is usually marked by a change of location or place or by the exit of a character.

–   A change of scene should advance the plot and our knowledge of character: it should be as short or as long as it takes to do this.

In a TV or film drama, much of the information about character and plot is carried by images which can move the story on very rapidly. Because television and film are able to tell a story by cutting from image to image, scenes, at least as they appear in the printed script, tend to be short.

Take, as an example, four brief images:

–   a child's foot kicks a ball into the road;

–   a close-up of a car speedometer shows the needle touching sixty;

–   a foot pumps hard on a brake peddle;

–   the child steps off the kerb to the sound of squealing tyres.

We don't need any more information to know what is happening. We certainly don't need a commentary to tell us.

One of the commonest mistakes made by writers new to television is to write far too much. They want to spell everything out in minute detail so that viewers don't miss anything. In fact, this has the opposite effect and makes things far too complicated. We are all very accomplished readers of the visual image and we can absorb an astonishing amount of information very quickly; we don't need to be told everything.

EXERCISE

The aim of this exercise is to exploit the necessary brevity of the typical television scene in order:

- to encourage pupils to identify and develop the dramatically essential elements in what they write.

This exercise takes one of the staple scenes of the soap: two characters arguing about the state of their relationship. Let us suppose that one partner has been waiting at home for the other, who now comes in late.

Ask the class to write the scene from the moment the front door opens until the argument ends. Encourage them to write as much as possible and leave nothing out that might help the audience understand the nature of this relationship.

Read the results, looking in particular for scenes which take a long time to get going, like this:

JO: Hullo.

DAVE: Hi.

JO: I'm home.

DAVE: Yeah.

JO: Something wrong?

DAVE: No.

JO: You sure?

DAVE: Yes.

JO: You're being a bit odd.

DAVE: Am I?

JO: You annoyed?

DAVE: You said you'd be in early.

JO: Look ...

DAVE: Don't bother trying to explain.

If possible, photocopy examples and ask the class, working in pairs, to mark what they think are the most important lines in the scene. The point they are looking for is that moment when the verbal sparring stops and the drama starts. This is not at all an easy thing to do and ought to stimulate some debate about what might be necessary to the drama and what might not.

Once they have reached a decision, tell them to edit out all the rest of the dialogue and retain only the lines they think essential to the drama. The scenes should now be read again and the results compared and discussed.

It should be pointed out that the purpose of this experiment is not to prove that one doesn't have to write very much in order to make a play: quite the reverse. What one must be able to do is to sense what is worth keeping and what can be cut. That means learning to recognise the moment when the drama is happening.

In the above example, we don't need to see Jo coming in and we don't really want all the waffle that gets the scene going. Much more effective would be a plunge into the heart of the argument:

DAVE: You think I like behaving like this?

JO: Probably.

DAVE: So you wouldn't mind if I stayed out all night? Didn't call?

It's not great drama, but at least it's not treating the audience like fools; it's leaving some work for them to do and it's getting straight into the action. Similarly, at the end of the scene the audience doesn't need to see our two lovers making up or swearing undying love. That can be done with a single line of dialogue:

JO: I don't want to be on my own tonight.

A half-hour TV play may need to create an impression of non-stop activity, vivid characterisation and dramatic incident all in the space of twenty-five minutes. How can it possibly do this?

The most useful piece of advice I have had was to be told to 'join every scene after it's started and leave it before it ends.' In other words, start the scene after it would realistically have started and leave it before it would realistically have ended. Cut out everything that is extraneous to the drama, identify the essence of the scene and go straight for it.

The point about brevity is important, because we want to encourage pupils to look for what is important in their writing and concentrate their efforts on that. This is the essence of drafting: it should be an opportunity for pupils to experiment and improve, not to perfect their handwriting.

Follow-up suggestions

1.   Take a previously written scene, perhaps from an earlier exercise, and tell the class to be ruthless; cut out as many lines as they can from the beginning and as many lines from the end while still keeping the sense. Discuss the result.

2.   Alternatively, take the last lines of a scene and put them first and use the opening lines at the end. It might be a disaster but, if it is, the original will still be there in the morning. Nothing will have been lost, and a useful insight might have been gained.

3.   Take a scene involving a boy and a girl: try swapping the lines over and give the boy's lines to the girl, and the girl's lines to the boy. Try the same technique with a villain and a hero, an old man and a young woman, a white person and a non-white person, etc.

8. SHIFTING SYMPATHIES

In drama, as in life, character and story can never be separated. The sort of person you are causes you to do certain things: the things that happen to you cause you to become a different kind of person. A play tries to show this process as it happens. If, as we have been told, drama is character in action, then what we expect from a play is to see people doing things and changing in the process.

Any change in a character will also affect the audience's perception of a character. A playwright uses this knowledge consciously, manipulating the sympathies of the audience by shifting their sympathies from one character to another. This is one way in which good plays avoid two-dimensional characters and allow characters to change, develop and surprise the audience, in the same way as people do in real life.

EXERCISE

The aims of this exercise are:

- to explore the interplay between character and plot
- to show pupils how plays 'manipulate' audiences.

Tell the class that character A wants to borrow some money from B; B, however, doesn't intend to part with any money. This must be borne in mind as the single most important factor motivating our characters. It is what they want.

Ask pupils to write the scene, trying to make us, the audience, sympathetic towards B and unsympathetic towards A. In other words, they must try to get the audience on B's side by making his case as persuasive as they can.

Next, ask them to write a second scene, in which it is revealed that the situation is not quite as simple as we had supposed. A, we now discover, needs the money for an operation, and B has plenty in the bank. This should involve shifting the sympathies of the audience so that they are now with A and against B.

Pupils should now have two short scenes, between which our feelings towards the characters change as a result of what we have learned about them.

Now ask pupils to write a third scene. In this, we discover two things: A has a reputation for being untrustworthy and bad with money and he has let people down in the past. B may have money in the bank, but only because his house burned down and he collected an insurance claim. Following this scene, our sympathy should be back with B again.

This process can be continued by constantly revealing more and more layers of information about A and B so that they become more complex and more interesting, e.g.:

- Character A might be bad with money, but B burned the house down himself for the insurance.

- A might have done some stupid things with money, but that was ten years ago when he was just a kid.

- B might have set fire to his house for the insurance, but this was because, having lost his job, he faced financial ruin.

The important thing is to try to keep the sympathies of the audience swinging from one to the other and back again. At each stage, pupils should be encouraged to examine their methods and discuss what has been achieved.

The movement of sympathy from one character to another that we have tried to cram into a single scene is an example, in miniature, of what it might take a playwright a whole play to achieve. It takes time for the audience to get to know a character, and the playwright might want to develop one aspect fully before allowing us to see another.

9. POSTSCRIPT

The trouble with trying to formulate a set of even very vague 'principles' for playwriting (as some experts in television and film have tried to do) is that you soon discover that all the most powerful and affecting plays you have ever seen break those rules. Howard Brenton says, 'There are two rules of aesthetics in the theatre. First rule: there are no rules. Second rule: because of the first rule, there cannot be a second.'

At the start of this book, I talked about the need to surprise yourself with what you write. Most of the exercises have been designed to help you teach others how to do that for themselves. Writing is, for most of us, a solitary activity. No matter how much support we have from our partners, script editors and directors, we are working on our own. However, the loneliness of writing is more than compensated for by those moments when we make a discovery or find a fresh and exciting way of saying something. Some people seem to have original ideas all the time, but for most of us it's plain hard work. To write well, you have to want to do it more than anything else. Pupils have to know that.

In this book, I have tried to describe how some of the skills of the dramatist might be acquired and practised. We began with snatches of conversation, fragments of speech, and ended with exercises in which we attempted the difficult task of manipulating the feelings and sympathies of an audience.

A play, however, is an artificial thing deliberately fashioned to tell a story, teach us something, move us to laughter, rage and tears or simply console us for the pain of being human. All drama, if it is to be successful, must be grounded in this life we share and cannot stop talking about.

In Berthold Brecht's poem, 'On the Everyday Theatre', he calls upon dramatic artists, playwrights and actors, to remember always where their work begins:

> You who perform plays
> In great houses under electric suns
> Before silent faces, pay a visit sometimes
> To the theatre whose stage is the street.
> The everyday, thousandfold, fameless theatre,

Common, unrewarded with honour,
But vivid, earthy, living,
Fed by the traffic of daily human contact.
The theatre whose stage is the street.

We are the only creatures that, in Toni Morrison's phrase, 'do language'. It is, perhaps our greatest evolutionary advantage over other creatures, and all of us have the power to make it vigorous and compelling. Most of us, however, only ever achieve this in moments of great crisis, or when our world is rearranged painfully and dramatically by tragedy and loss. Then our words, shorn of the stammering clichés of everyday life, can achieve a beautiful and terrible simplicity. It is the task of the writer to make this happen every day and on every page.

Bibliography

Austin, J. L. *How to do Things with Words*, OUP
Brecht, B. *On the Everyday Theatre* Methuen
DES (1975), *A Language for Life* (the report of the committee of inquiry –
   chairman, Sir Alan Bullock), HMSO
Naipaul, V. S. (1987), *The Enigma of Arrival*, Viking
Pinter, H. (1958), *The Dumb Waiter*, French
Priestley, J. B. (1965), *An Inspector Calls*, Heinemann
Steinbeck, J. (1966), *Of Mice and Men*, Heinemann